How to Fulfill Your Potential

How to Fulfill Your Potential

Physical, Emotional, and Spiritual Harmony

From the Success in Christian Living series—a practical approach to achieving your goals for time, money, motivation, and human potential.

by Dennis E. Hensley

Published by Warner Press
Anderson, Indiana

Copyright ©1989 by Warner Press, Inc.
and Dennis E. Hensley
ISBN 0-87162-477-X
All Rights Reserved
Printed in the United States of America
Warner Press, Inc.
Arlo F. Newell, Editor in Chief
Dan Harman, Book Editor
Caroline Smith, Editor

Contents

Contents

Part 1:
Here Comes the
Dreamer!

I n Genesis 37:1-6 we read the story of a young man named named Joseph who had dreams and visions of future events. When he shared these dreams with other people, he expected them to value his insight and to follow his advice and leading. After all, didn't it seem logical to make plans for the future based on advance knowledge of what was to transpire?

Unfortunately, Joseph's youthful naiveté made him unaware of how envy, greed, suspicion, and anger can make people blind to the truth. He did not understand one consistent weakness of the human character: **people only want to know about what the future holds when the predictions are for better times ahead.**

Not understanding this flaw in human nature, Joseph openly revealed his dreams to everyone around him. This led to disaster. When he told his brothers that he dreamed they would one day bow before him, the brothers kidnapped him and sold him into slavery, reporting to their father that their brother had been killed. In prison later, Joseph interpreted a dream in which one of pharaoh's servants would be restored to service and the other would be killed. When these two events transpired, Joseph was alienated from his fellow inmates. Hundreds of years later, Christ would explain that prophets cannot be taken seriously by those living close to them (Luke 4:24).

Despite these setbacks, Joseph was eventually able to triumph over adversity. He was exonerated of his crime, released from prison, made a chief advisor to the pharaoh, proclaimed a national hero, and indeed he saw his brothers bow before him as he had predicted so many years before.

Certainly the guiding hand of God was actively leading in Joseph's life. Whatever **problem** was thrown at Joseph, he looked to God to open an **opportunity** so that good would result in spite of the situation. As Joseph later explained to his brothers concerning their action of selling him into slavery, "You meant evil against me; but God meant it for good" (Genesis 50:20).

Truly, the Holy Spirit was leading Joseph in the direction God wanted the young man to take. But we must remember that the Holy Spirit was not **forcing** Joseph into a set of righteous steps. As with you and me, Joseph was a person of free will. He was not a robot that God would wind up or pre-program to behave in a guaranteed manner. Joseph honored God by **choosing** to do what was pleasing and acceptable to the Lord.

Knowing this, it behooves us to reexamine Joseph's life in order to discover what the factors were that led to his ultimate success. What can we learn about him that we can emulate and thereby also bring success into our own lives? That is the topic of Part 1.

Chapter 1:

Joseph Dreamed a Dream

U nless you have a dream you can't make a dream come true. You have to take first things first. That's what Joseph did. God gave him a vision to become a great and useful person, and Joseph accepted that vision as a worthy goal for his life. He began with a dream.

Unlike Daniel, Jeremiah, and John the Revelator, young Joseph was not considered to be a prophet. He was not called to walk the streets in sackcloth, wailing and chanting predictions of impending doom. He was simply a person to whom God had given a mission (to honor God before a pagan nation) and one gift (to interpret dreams). The rest of the responsibility was his.

This has not changed today, even though many would-be churchgoers would like to think so. Upon accepting Christ as our Savior, we were given special gifts and talents from God (Romans 12:6, 1 Corinthians 12:4, 2 Timothy 1:6). As with Joseph, we should be using these gifts to honor God—even though God will not force us to do so. Similarly, we all need a dream of something extraordinary we can make come true as a gift of service to God.

Christians do not need a Jacob's-ladder or Road-to-Damascus experience in order to develop a dream or vision of something noble they can do to serve the Lord. Opportunities for great service, often disguised as great problems, arise continually. Our decision must be to grab the dream, as Joseph did, or reject it, as his brothers did. As George Bernard Shaw once wrote, "People who get on in this world are the people who get up and look for the circumstances they want, and, if they can't find them, make them."

I must confess that I was slow in learning this. I, too, felt that the great leaders—the visionaries—for Christ had to begin by hearing a voice from a burning bush or by seeing a sheet lowered from heaven. I learned differently, however.

In my case, I had been praying for the Lord to call me to do something extraordinary for his glory. I had served in the church in a dozen or more capacities, and these were all activities that honored the Lord and served the church. Still, I had a personal desire to do at least one absolutely incredible thing during my lifetime solely for God's glory. This was my dream.

After praying this way for several months, an opportunity presented itself that I felt might possibly provide a way for me to do a magnificent service to God. Our church's Christian elementary school was $10,000 in debt. The members of the school board wanted to raise an endowment fund that would counterbalance this debt with positive cashflow. I was asked to spearhead this effort, and I accepted the challenge.

The thought occurred to me that, whereas a fund-raising effort of $10,000 would make the school financially solvent again, an effort to raise $100,000 would make it solvent for many years to come. I wondered if the Lord would be willing to call me forth to raise this amount.

I began to pray earnestly that God would show me a sign to prove to me that this dream of mine was within God's perfect will. In my heart I knew it was a noble thing to do; in my soul I felt it was a righteous goal to have; in my mind I determined it to be a helpful and logical way to assist the school. Nevertheless, I wanted proof positive that God was pleased with my ambitions and that God sanctioned this dream of mine. So, I prayed for a sign and I did absolutely no work in relation to establishing an endowment fund for the school.

Hours, days, and weeks passed. I watched for writing in the clouds. I listened for God's voice to speak amidst the thunderstorm. I laid in bed awaiting the arrival of an angel.

Nothing happened.

So I continued to pray. And God continued to withhold a miraculous sign. I prayed more. And waited more. Still nothing happened.

Finally, in exhaustion one night, as I was half-praying and half-drifting off to sleep, I remember thinking, Lord, please let me try to raise this $100,000 for your ministry to children. Please let me do this, Lord.

And deep in the recesses of my mind, a very basic response gently came to me: "So who's stopping you?"

Instantly, my eyes popped open and I almost started to laugh. What a simple and obvious thing to discover. I sat up in bed and slapped my forehead in amazement. Why had I been trying to make a very fundamental matter of Christian service into something so complicated and ethereal? If I had a dream of serving the Lord in a great way and then an opportunity arose by which I could do so, wouldn't it seem logical for me to get busy instead of challenging God to pat me on the head and brag about my personal holiness?

I suddenly realized that my prayers had been all wrong. I had been praying for the opportunity to do something great for God, and then I had been waiting for God to promise to do all the work so that I could come off looking like a hero. How ridiculous! The whole purpose of doing service for God is **to do it for God!**

That very night I began to make plans for instituting the endowment fund for the school. I recruited other helpers, including one retired person who had been a fundraiser for a Christian college. The first year we raised the needed $10,000. The next year we doubled that to $20,000. The third year we doubled that to $40,000. The fund kept increasing until we reached our goal of $100,000. Shortly thereafter, we surpassed $150,000.

In our enthusiasm to serve the Lord, we were able to exceed even our wildest dreams of success. But **first** we had to dream the dream before we could make the dream come true.

"Small opportunities are often the beginnings of great enterprises."
—Demosthenes

Chapter 2:

Joseph Did Not Waver

Dreams are wonderful if the dream ultimately comes true. This can happen only if you determine to keep focused on the one dream you have chosen for yourself and if you keep pursuing it despite the setbacks and challenges.

Joseph's dream called for him to rise to a position of great political power so that he could use his rank and prestige to make the greatness of God known to many. In striving to fulfill his dream, Joseph was confronted by many problems. He was kidnaped, beaten, sold into slavery, falsely accused of attempted rape, put in prison, mocked, ridiculed, and isolated. Through it all, he continued to pray, work, and move closer to fulfilling his destiny.

To keep myself focused on the dream of raising $100,000 and more for the school endowment fund, I reminded myself constantly of what my dream was. This included my preparing frequent progress reports to the supporters of the fund, charts to mark our advances, and a billboard in our school foyer to publicize the fund. I talked about the fund to everyone I met. I even wrote and published a small tract on how to donate to the fund.

People who stray from their predetermined paths usually lose time, energy, and confidence. No matter how slow the progress may seem to be, it's still genuine progress if it moves you closer to your goal.

Vince Lombardi once referred to football as "a game of inches." By that he meant that kicking a 50-yard field goal for three points was not as important as being able to carry the football that last inch over the goal line for six points. First downs and touchdowns were earned an inch at a time through head-to-head confrontation on the line of scrimmage.

Life is often that way, too. As each day passes, you are a winner if you've moved even an inch (or a dollar or a person or a pound) closer to your ultimate dream fulfillment. Persistence is the key to great success. You must have a dream and then never waver in pursuing it.

Chapter 3:

Joseph Allied Himself with Other Dreamers

Working alone, a person with a dream and a lot of determination can achieve his or her goal. The problem is that doing it alone takes an abnormally long time. If one person with a vision of success can work in tandem with one or more other persons with equal visions of success, the synergy (simultaneous energy) makes the success come much sooner.

In Daniel Defoe's classic novel *Robinson Crusoe*, the main character works for a dozen years trying to reshape the island he is living on. He makes some great strides, but he also is limited in how much one person can accomplish. After he meets the cannibal Friday and befriends him, the two begin working together. In short order, major changes are made to the island—canals are dug, fortress walls erected, rocks moved. Two people working together at lifting, balancing, digging, and pushing were more powerful than three working separately.

This proved true for Joseph, too. He predicted to the Egyptian pharaoh that seven years of good rain would be followed by seven years of drought. The pharaoh believed in Joseph's vision for the future. He ordered him to store grain during the bountiful years so that no one would starve during the lean years.

When I began to raise money for the school endowment fund, I told my dream of raising $100,000 to Harold Ranes, a retired minister who had once served eight years as director of fund-raising at Fort Wayne Bible College. Harold caught the vision I had for our school, and he became my partner in the effort. While I made financial appeals to parents, grand-parents, and neighbors of the students in our school, Harold called on businesses, corporations, and foundations to seek donations. Often one or the other of us would secure a new donation every few days. Each new success spurred us to keep working toward our ultimate goal.

Harold died on March 1, 1988, at the age of 82. Even though we had secured far more money than our original $100,000 goal, the last time I talked with Harold he made two sug-gestions to me concerning how we could raise even more money for the school's endowment fund. He never lost the vision.

Strength is multiplied and magnified in numbers. King David raised a large army to defend the nation. Gideon fought with three hundred hand-chosen soldiers. Noah's sons worked with him in building the ark. Christ traveled with twelve disciples. Paul traveled with Barnabas and Silas on missionary journeys.

Once you establish your worthy dream, seek others who will work with you in making it come true. The fellowship, support, and additional strength you gain will be just what you need to keep you working toward your goal.

Part 2:

The Power of Persistence

We noted earlier that Joseph succeeded because he never wavered from his dream. This is the only common denominator you will find among all successful people: **they refuse to give up.** It is a quality that is apparent in all great leaders.

Think that through for a moment and you will realize how true it really is. For example, you cannot say that all great leaders are physically attractive. For every handsome John F. Kennedy, you will find a dozen homely Abe Lincolns, bald Winston Churchills, and plain Golda Meirs. You cannot sight physical strength either, since Franklin Roosevelt was crippled by polio, Robert Dole was handicapped in his right arm by a war wound, and Julius Caesar suffered from epilepsy. Nor can you point to wealth either, since Andrew Carnegie arrived in America as a penniless immigrant, Benjamin Franklin began as a printer's assistant, and Ronald Reagan once worked as a five-dollar-per-week radio announcer in Iowa.

The only quality great leaders and successful people have in common is an internal motivation that makes them continue to strive toward their goal when others give up and quit. Joseph was sold into slavery, but he stayed focused on his dream. He was framed by Potiphar's wife and returned to prison, but he still remembered his destiny. He faced one setback after another, but he never forgot his goal. Eventually, he obtained it.

Anyone with that sort of persistence is bound to succeed. No barriers are too great to be overcome if a person has adequate motivation and determination.

Chapter 4:

People Who
Were Persistent

History is replete with people who persisted through great odds to reach their goals. Helen Keller became deaf and blind at nineteen months of age. She found a motivating force in her teacher Anne Sullivan. Helen determined to be the equal of any person without handicaps. At age twenty Helen graduated *cum laude* from Radcliffe College at Harvard University with special honors in English literature as well as in French and German languages. At twenty-one she wrote her autobiography. Later, she also wrote *Helen Keller's Journal*. Any impairments she may have had were more than compensated for by her ambition, drive, and persistence.

George Meegan spent seven years walking 19,017 miles from the southernmost tip of South America to the northernmost tip of Alaska. He is listed in the *Guinness Book of World Records* for having completed in 1977 the longest continuous walking trip. When interviewed about this amazing and bizarre stunt, Meegan said, "I never thought of it as two continents. I only focused on the mile immediately ahead of me. If I ever became discouraged, I'd remind myself that I had already walked thousands of miles, so one more mile would be easy. Finally, the walk was over."

Struggles are not always bad. A little boy who loved nature once opened a cocoon in order to help a butterfly come out. The butterfly died. The little boy did not understand that the struggle to get out was what strengthened and matured the butterfly.

My own father, L. Edward Hensley, was a living example of persistence for me as I grew up. He knew even as a young boy that he would one day be successful in business, despite the fact that everything seemed stacked against him. His father contracted tuberculosis at an early age, forcing my father to quit school after the eighth grade in order to support his parents and little sister. He picked cotton in ninety-degree heat in Tennessee and watched cars drive by on a nearby road. There and then he made a vow to himself that he would do whatever it took to escape the cotton fields and one day drive down that road in a fancy car of his own.

At age fifteen he traveled north to Detroit where he ran a newsstand in a bank by day and finished his high school education by night. At seventeen he enlisted in the navy and did sea duty in Central and South America. At eighteen he married my mother and at twenty they bought our first home. I was born later that year. My father started his own optical business, but it was not a great success. Later, he formed a new optical business with three partners, but it went bankrupt. Despite all this, he still maintained his dream of becoming successful in business.

Although he had to drive a cab at nights to help support us as well as work in someone else's optical grinding lab for a regular job, he found time to read books, attend conventions, and carefully follow the trade magazines. During the late 1950s he concentrated his studies on a newly developing product called "contact lenses." Most other opticians thought they were a gimmick item, something that would be forgotten within two or three years. But not my father. He predicted a time when millions of people would be wearers of contact lenses. He formed the Phoenix Contact Lens Company on borrowed money and, in time, became so successful he was able to buy out all of his silent partners. He renamed the business the Hensley Contact Lens Company. Later, he formed a subsidiary optical lens business and then a prosthetic eye laboratory. He bought his own building and hired several employees to work for him.

After his businesses were going well, he bought a Lincoln

Continental automobile. He took my mother, brother, sister, and me on a trip to Camden, Tennessee, where he had lived as a boy and had picked cotton. We all drove down the road near the cotton fields and my father smiled and said, "At last! At last!" It was a personal triumph made possible only by undaunted persistence.

>0-0-0-0-0-0-0-0-0-0-0-0-0-0-0-0-0-0-0-0-0-0-0-0-0-0-0<

*"If you have built castles
in the air, your work
need not be lost;
that is where they
should be. Now put
foundations under them."*
—Henry David Thoreau

>0-0-0-0-0-0-0-0-0-0-0-0-0-0-0-0-0-0-0-0-0-0-0-0-0-0-0<

Chapter 5:

The Common Denominator of Successful People

George Eliot once wrote, "It is never too late to be what you might have been." I like the optimistic nature of that quotation. It reminds me of the fact that sometimes that last tiny measure of persistence makes all the difference between winning and losing. Roger Maris became baseball's all-time home-run champion by hitting just one more home run than Babe Ruth had hit in a single season. Roger Bannister became the first person in the world to break the four-minute mile. His speed of 3 minutes and 59.4 seconds was less than a 1 percent improvement over world-record-holder Gunder Haegg of Sweden, whose best time was 4 minutes and 1.4 seconds. When A.J. Foyt won the Indianapolis 500 race in 1961, he was only five seconds faster than second-place winner Eddie Sacks—despite the fact the race lasted more than three-and-a-half hours. In each example, a tiny bit of extra effort made all the difference.

You may wonder whether or not it's worth putting forth that extra effort to achieve your dream. That point is not even debatable. You must do your best, give your all, reach your goal. If you don't, you'll be condemning yourself to a life of misery. Bob Conklin, author of *Adventures in Attitudes*, explains, "Deep within your consciousness is the realization that your life has a purpose, a destiny, a meaning which must be discovered. Until this is achieved, you will experience boredom, dissatisfaction, frustration, and the feeling of hunger or despair."

When we try to pretend that our lives lack special purpose, we thwart the inner-guidance system that God has installed in us to direct us toward a joyful satisfaction in the fulfillment of our potential. Indeed, personal destiny can be a scary thing to confront. Jonah ran in a different direction. Noah tried to drink himself into a stupor with alcohol. Peter tried to deny his role as a disciple of Christ. The eight cowardly spies tried to turn from entering the Promised Land. For each one, the judgment of God was harsh, but the feeling of personal failure may have been even worse: each one had to live with the knowledge that he had been a disappointment not only to God but also to himself. And just as you can never outrun God, you likewise can never outrun yourself. Stay the course. Be a winner, not a loser.

That old hymn "Give of Your Best to the Master" contains a call for excellence in serving Christ. People admire those who give their best, who lead the field in whatever their calling is. The simple fact is that no matter how extraordinary your accomplishment is, if you aren't first or best it carries very little impact. Let me prove this to you.

In my seminars on motivation, I conduct a survey during my lectures. I ask the participants to raise their hands if they know who Charles Duke is. To date, no one has ever put up a hand. Then I ask them to raise their hands if they know who Neil Armstrong is. Every hand goes up. I then explain that only ten people in the history of the world have ever set foot on the moon. Charles Duke was number nine—but who cares? No matter how extraordinary your accomplishment is, if you don't strive for absolute excellence it may still leave you in an also-ran status.

Some Christians will argue that striving to be a successful person draws too much glory on themselves. That is a cop-out. When Joseph became the second-most-powerful person in Egypt, his position gave him a greater chance to proclaim the might and glory of the one true God. When Paul set out to be the first evangelist in Macedonia, he pioneered a whole new region for Christianity. Their persistence in rising to the pinnacle of their personal-achievement limits allowed them to be of maximum service to God.

What about you? Are you an also-ran or a leader? Begin now to persist toward excellence.

-:=:=:=:=:=:=:=:=:=:=:=:=:=:=:=:=:=:=:=:-

**"It's not your aptitude
but your <u>attitude</u>
that determines
your altitude."
—Reverend Jesse Jackson**

-:=:=:=:=:=:=:=:=:=:=:=:=:=:=:=:=:=:=:=:-

Part 3:
Making Weaknesses
into Strengths

W hile watching a documentary about the battle for
North Africa in World War II, I noted their observation that the British changed their tactical com-
manders time and again, searching for the right leader for that
battlefront. The Germans, however, kept the same commander
year after year: Field Marshall Erwin Rommel.

The British were supported by Allied soldiers from India,
Australia, New Zealand, Poland, France, and Canada. They
vastly outnumbered the Germans. Moreover, the Germans
were low on supplies of food, ammunition, and gasoline.
Despite these overwhelming handicaps, the Germans continued to win victory after victory. The key to their success
was the use of tactics unknown to the British.

Rommel knew that, though the British were large in force
and supplies, they used old-fashioned and bogged-down
methods. Not so the Germans. They had devised faster tanks,
new battlefield strategies, and better methods of communication. Being small did not make them weaker; it only made
them more alert to opportunities.

When the British laid down a vast mine field to prevent the
Germans from attacking them head-on, the Germans realized
that this also blocked the British on one side. Knowing that
the sea was behind the British, the Germans made a rapid end
run around the mine field and attacked the British in a
squeeze play. The British didn't realize that fighting could be
done with such speed and aggression. They were caught
totally unprepared.

Rommel's techniques for waging a desert war made him ruler of 1400 miles of North African territory for a time. When a German tank was damaged, the Germans would come back during the night and retrieve it, repair it, and use it again. When the Germans would stage an assault on the British, the British would retreat to a fall-back position of safety. When the British would attack the Germans, the Germans would use long range anti-tank guns to disrupt the attack and then they would use that time of confusion as a chance to mount a counterattack and rout the British.

This went on continuously. Not until the Allies started to emulate Rommel's tactics were they ever able to get the upper hand on the Germans. And even then, many analysts feel that if Rommel had had adequate supplies, he still would have defeated the Allies.

This lesson from history indicates that innovation is far more valuable than tradition. No matter how large a business, church, or organization is, it cannot afford to become static. If it does, one day a small competitor with an innovative idea will come along and put an end to the larger entity.

Chapter 6:

The Key Is Innovation

History is replete with the stories of innovators:

- When Edison discovered a filament for the light-bulb, it eliminated the whale oil trade within four years.
- When Henry Ford devised a way of producing automobiles that were affordable to every American, more than 93 percent of all blacksmiths went out of business.
- When Knute Rockne devised the forward pass in football, none of the teams who competed against Notre Dame could defeat them.
- When Al Jolson sang and talked in "The Jazz Singer," more than thirty studios producing silent films went out of business within eighteen months.
- When Panasonic created the transistor radio, the entire console-tube radio business was ended in less than a year's time.
- When Seiko developed the quartz watch, more than twenty Swiss and American watch companies—some that had been in business more than 150 years—went bankrupt.
- When U.S. Air devised its low-price no-frills passenger service, Continental Airlines and several other large airlines either filed for bankruptcy or merged with other airlines in order to survive.

I could give numerous additional examples of how giants have been felled by seemingly weaker opponents or competitors. In each success story the key factor was innovation.

Many Christians fail to reach their full potential because they automatically eliminate themselves from competing with an already established entity. That's too bad, because the farther down you begin, the easier it is to show progress.

The world of business has proved this point frequently. When Avis Rent-A-Car wanted to compete with number-one-rated Hertz, the Avis ads stated, "We're Number Two, So We Try Harder." The truth was that Avis was the number-six-rated car rental company at that time. Within six months, however, Avis actually rose to number two. That increased its business almost four-fold. We may question the ethics of their ad slogan; nevertheless the results are not bad for a "little guy."

Finding competition with Pepsi-Cola and Coca-Cola ever more difficult, 7-Up decided to turn its apparent weakness into a strength. It launched an advertising campaign that bragged about the fact that 7-Up was the "Un-Cola." It stressed the "clear, clean taste" and reminded people that as far as caffeine was concerned, "7-Up never had it, never will." Soon, sales of 7-Up were at an all-time high.

What happened in these two instances was that the companies themselves refused to accept a low position. They determined to be contenders. They set their own value and worth, and then they worked to make it evident to everyone else.

What sort of value have you set on yourself? Potential is there for greatness within you, but if you don't recognize it first, no one else will, either. A man once handed a five-pound iron bar to his son and asked him how much it was worth. The boy said he didn't know. The father then told the boy that it was worth whatever potential it was raised to. As a five-pound doorstop, it was worth two dollars; reshaped into horseshoes, it would be worth ten dollars; formed into sewing needles it would be worth $1,000; and melted down and recast as surgical scalpels it would be worth $10,000. The value of an item and the value of an individual are both determined by what their final development is.

When I was in high school, I had a friend named Dexter Waverly who had a crush on a pretty cheerleader named Ashley Becker. Dexter wore glasses and was barely five-feet-six. Athletically, he was no match for the varsity basketball and football players who usually asked Ashley out on dates. He decided, nevertheless, that he was going to make Ashley his steady girl friend.

Dexter knew his shortcomings, and so he did not try to join sports teams. He competed in areas where the odds were more in his favor. When Ashley took French in eleventh grade, so did Dexter. He sat near her in class and helped her after school with her homework. They both joined the French club and Dexter was elected its president. Later that year when Ashley mentioned that she was going to try out for the annual school drama production, Dexter won a role, too, and he met with Ashley to study their lines. When Ashley volunteered to spend one of her study hall periods working as an assistant in the library, Dexter volunteered, too.

By the end of the year, Ashley decided that she had a lot more in common with Dexter than she did with the varsity players who took her out on dates and spent the whole evening talking about hook shots or end runs. By the time our senior year rolled around, Dexter and Ashley were dating exclusively. They later decided to attend the same college. Today, Dexter is a middle-school principal and his wife, Ashley, is a fifth-grade teacher in the same building. Every time I see them at our class reunions, I am still amazed that that guy was really able to marry that girl. It's one of the most inspiring examples of turning minuses into plusses that I've ever seen. Dexter set a high value on his own worth to Ashley, and he then set to work to make it evident to her. The plan worked.

Naturally, we would be naive to think that in every circumstance our weaknesses could be turned into strengths. But in situations where more strength is needed, we should be willing to commit the time to enhance our abilities. Arnold Schwarzenegger won five world-bodybuilding championships. When asked what the secret to his success was, he answered, "My competitors tried to make their strongest points even stronger. Instead, I spent most of my time on my weakest areas. When I got my entire body on an equally strong basis, the judges decided I was closer to perfect than someone who had bigger biceps yet disproportionately smaller legs."

During the nine years I spent working on staff at three different colleges, I gave similar advice to the students I worked with. If they wanted to win a scholarship or get named to the dean's list, I would tell them not to try to go from an A- to an A+ in English, but instead to concentrate on going from a C- to a B+ in physics. We all have weak areas; what's encouraging is that they don't have to remain that way. We can read, study, ask questions, travel, attend seminars, join support groups, listen to tapes and records, watch informative television, video-cassettes, and motion-picture productions, and even experiment on our own. Improvement is always possible, always necessary.

How to Dream a Dream and Make It Come True

1. **Don't let the masses convince you that your dream is impossible.** They may be wrong and you might be right. Orville and Wilbur Wright were told that no one could possibly fly in a heavier-than-air machine. Roger Bannister was told that no one could run a mile in less than four minutes. Donald Trump was told that a person under thirty couldn't earn a billion dollars. They did it anyway. They believed in themselves and in their destinies.

2. **Devise a game plan for achieving your goal.** Be specific in outlining the steps of progress you will need to make in order to reach your goal. Consider time frames, expenses, outside commitments, personnel, and equipment. If your goal is to build your dream house during the next year, break the construction into twelve monthly objectives, each with four weekly tasks, and each of those with five daily projects. Keep on schedule and you'll complete your home.

3. **Plan to work a lot of overtime.** No one ever gets ahead by working a basic eight-hour day. If you worked two forty-hour work weeks every seven days, that would still leave you eighty-eight hours of discretionary time. Not to tap into these extra hours is to waste one of your most valuable resources: time!

**"Life is like the movies.
We produce our own show."**
—Mark Todd

Chapter 7:

A Matter of Perspective

I was once hired by an insurance company to help motivate its employees to work harder and sell more policies. Prior to my series of lectures, I took time to meet the sales-people I would be addressing. I discovered that most of them enjoyed their jobs and liked working for the company they were with. Some had been salespersons or general agents for nearly twenty years. They were comfortable and content, and they wanted things to go along the way they always had. Maintaining the status quo was fine with them.

Unfortunately, a larger company had recently acquired the insurance company, and progress was now the byword in everything. Sales quotas were increased; territories were ex-panded; new product lines were introduced. Word had come down from top management that a six-month grace period would be offered to all carry-over employees. After that time, however, those who could not meet the rigid new standards of the company would either be retired or fired. My job was to try to help the complacent employees develop a new zest for sales work.

After talking with the employees, I discovered that their company's previous owner had done them a disservice by not challenging them to improve themselves as each year passed. One woman told me that she had always intented to attend night school to earn an MBA degree, but when nobody at the company seemed to care one way or the other about it, she just gave up on the idea. Another woman told me that she had a sales territory that had a strong Italian ethnic heritage in every neighborhood. She knew that if she could just learn to speak Italian, she could increase her sales immeasurably. But she just never seemed to find enough time to hire a language tutor or to attend a summer course to learn the language.

Other people had similar stories—one felt that he should learn more about computers, another thought he should learn how to sell policies to college students, another thought she should become more knowledgeable about how insurance could help in estate planning. Each case, however, was lacking enough time or money or incentive to follow through on these good intentions.

I recognized instantly that the main problem here was one of perspective. All of these people felt that personal self-improvement would only benefit the company and not the salesperson. They didn't realize that each time a person overcomes a weakness or enhances a developing skill, he or she has become a greater individual than was the case the day before. Having more talent subsequently leads to having more confidence. That, in turn, leads to gaining more success—success for both the company **and** the worker.

This became the point of emphasis in all my lectures and my one-on-one meetings with employees. Soon the insurance agents came to realize that there was no such thing as maintaining the status quo. Either persons were advancing in their careers or they were falling behind. The shock of this realization shook them out of their nonchalance. After that, learning how to become competitive became serious business with them.

I gave each person a list of business books I felt should be read and studied. Before long, I saw these folks walking through the halls each day carrying a book under their arms. I also suggested they should use their driving time in cars as time to listen to instructional cassette tapes. This is how the one agent taught herself to speak Italian and the other agent learned the basics of estate planning.

Long before the six-month grace period was over, each

employee was making sales at or above the new quota requirements. Even better, a new sense of mission and an obvious charge of employee electricity pulsed through the company. Work became an enjoyable challenge as individuals became prouder of their new skills and subsequent sales accomplishments. Their home and personal lives were enhanced, too. And through it all, my only regret was that some of these fine people could have been enjoying these benefits all along, had they not shifted their self-development into neutral for two decades.

While working in the public-relations department at Manchester College, I took part in a survey that was being conducted jointly by students in the departments of psychology and business. We went to several area cities and stopped people on the street to ask them, "Would you like to be tremendously successful in your career?" Of 100 people surveyed, 94 said yes. We then asked, "Are you currently tremendously successful in your career?" Only two out of 100 answered yes.

This survey revealed that people did have a specific definition in their minds about what "tremendously successful" meant in their specific careers. Simultaneously, most of them felt that this ultimate success was not something they would ever achieve. They gave up before they ever began. They never had any idea of what their potential was because they had never explored it. What a shame.

People do not have to be second best at anything that is really important to them. In my state of Indiana there is an historic village called New Harmony. It was established during the 1850s by a native of Scotland named Robert Owen. New Harmony was known as a "village of cooperation" because it was created as a model socialist community. In theory, the settlers would all work equally hard and earn equal compensation and be equally content and happy. In practice, it was a chaotic mess that ultimately led to the failure of the experiment and the desertion of the people.

What is so ironic about the failure of New Harmony is that it was founded by a man who was an industrial capitalist in Scotland, one who made his fortune by realizing that all workers need incentive and motivation before they will work energetically. The key to instilling this motivation, Robert Owen discovered, was a sense of self-fulfillment through competition.

In 1809, Owen purchased a cotton mill that had gone to the edge of foreclosure under its previous management. After one week of ownership, Owen walked through his mill and tied red, green, or yellow ribbons on the factory machines. He announced that red meant above-average production, green meant routine production, and yellow meant poor production. He then left the factory for the day. He offered no bonus incentives for harder work; nor did he threaten to discharge anyone for doing substandard production. He just left the ribbons on and he walked away. Within sixty days every machine had a red ribbon. Production, quality, and morale were never higher.

For some odd reason, Robert Owen changed his mind late in life about the functional aspect of fair competition. He decided that the state of affairs of everyone would be improved if all people could be free to work as they pleased, yet be guaranteed a base of support. His entire life and career had taught him that this was not true; nevertheless, he invested his money in creating a model settlement in Indiana, but the model didn't endure its test run.

In Robert Owen's day, people needed to have a **reason** for wanting to do their best. Today, it seems to be no different. Owen motivated people by making a red ribbon an item of prestige. But what about the ninety-eight people in the Manchester College survey who were not "tremendously successful" in their careers because no Robert Owen had stepped forth to wave a red ribbon at them? What is their fate?

Simply put, they will **never** become successful until they realize the things we have discussed:

1. No obstacles are too great to overcome for the people who stay innovative.

2. Many times a weakness can become a strength if it is put in a new light.

3. Everyone has weak areas, but everyone has ways of making weak areas stronger.

4. Maintaining a competitive edge is what adds challenge and spark to life.

Use this insight to make yourself one of the two people who can say, Yes, I'm tremendously successful at what I do. And don't worry about failing: ninety-eight out of a hundred people aren't even trying.

Brainstorming: How to Generate Ideas

#1 Meet with a group of people, each with a different area of expertise. Notify everyone in advance of what the discussion topic will be and ask them to begin making notes about it.

#2 Begin the meeting by calling for all ideas to be shared, not judged, at first. Encourage people to be silly, bizarre, original, assertive, and imaginative. Try to come up with at least two dozen suggestions for dealing with the issue at hand.

#3 Enhance the list of ideas by blending one or two, eliminating the weakest ones, supplementing some with additional new thoughts, and evaluating the value of those remaining.

#4 Test the best ideas. If the tests work out, put the idea into full use.

Part 4:

Creative Discontent

An old joke tells of a man who said to his doctor, "Every time I lift my arm up like this it hurts me, Doc. What should I do?" The doctor responded, "Stop holding your arm up like that."

Ha, ha, ha, right? What's so funny about that?

Nothing actually—at least about the joke. What is funny, however, is that even though the response is so obvious, no one ever assumes it will be the answer. For this same reason, my guess is that people will still be asking the riddle of "Why did the chicken cross the road?" right up until the Lord returns.

In confronting problems, riddles, and puzzles, we never seem to think of the obvious solution. That's ridiculous, yet true.

Some years ago a cargo truck tried to pass under a low bridge and it became wedged against the overpass. The police and fire departments were called in, and for two hours the crew workers tried to pry and push and grease and nudge the truck loose. It wouldn't budge. Finally, a little boy who was walking by tugged on a police sergeant's sleeve and said, "Why don't ya let some air out of the tires?" Ten minutes later the truck was free.

In the popular Hans Christian Andersen story "The Emperor's New Clothes," a pompous king is told by two con artists that they have sewn a set of beautiful clothes made out of material that can be seen only by people who are not fools. Naturally, the king and everyone around him act as though they can see the clothes perfectly. A few days later, the king leads a parade through town. He is arrayed in the "new clothes" all the townspeople have heard so much about. They oooh and ahhh as he walks by in his underwear, each pretending to be able to see the outer clothes.

Finally, a young child looks at the king and breaks out laughing. He begins to scream, "The king has no clothes on! The king has no clothes on!" Within moments the entire crowd is chanting the same thing and laughing hysterically.

Adults never seem to see the obvious. One day a little girl innocently asked her mother, "Where do I come from?" With some degree of nervousness, the mother stumbled through a long discourse on love, sex, and childbirth. When she finished she asked her daughter if she had any questions. The little girl responded, "Yeah. I still want to know where I come from. Jenny said she came from Detroit, and I wanna know where I came from."

Christ told his followers that they needed the same sort of faith and innocence and honesty a child had if they intended to see the kingdom of God. Children are so wise it actually should embarrass us adults.

One day when my son Nathan was a first grader, he was leafing through a copy of the *National Geographic*. He noticed some pictures that an American jet pilot had taken of a Russian bomber when the bomber had come too close to American territory. Nathan asked me what the writing under the picture said, and so I tried to explain to him about the invasion of private territory and the threat of a hostile attack.

When I finished, Nathan said, "At school we have to sit in our own chair and keep 'hands off' our neighbor's chair and school supplies. Why don't the Americans and Russians just do 'hands off' too, dad?"

Not bad, eh? We spend billions on developing concepts to secure a strategic arms limitation pact and then a little kid comes up with an idea that in two minutes would solve all our problems. But, naw, that's too obvious.

Now that I'm past forty I find that I am turning more and more to "the obvious" as a way of doing my work as church officer, Sunday school teacher, and school board member.

Someone will say to me, "What should I do? My job just doesn't pay enough." My answer is, "Ask for a raise or get a second job."

Or they'll say, "My family life is dull and predictable. What should I do?" My answer is, "Try something exciting for a change."

Or, "My house is always a mess" and I'll respond, "Then clean it." Answers are so simple if you don't **try** to complicate them.

In earning my doctoral degree, I had to take more courses in educational psychology and philosophy of education than I care to remember. There were times back then when some of the theories I heard propounded actually caused me to laugh out loud. Researchers would take forty pages of textbook to explain something that I could summarize in one sentence.

In one instance, for example, our assignment was to read three chapters on research conclusions that had been drawn after years of analyzing human biorhythms. The professor called on me to summarize the chapters in class. I rose to my feet and said, "Cutting through all the hoopla, the bottom line is that different people work better at different times of day. And my old grandfather could have told you that and he doesn't know word one about scientific research." The class was dumbstruck by my candor, but the professor only said, "Excellent," and went to another question.

I have Christian friends who are strapped by a variety of problems. In talking with them I hear one phrase over and again: "I'm waiting for the Lord to show me what to do and then I'll do it." My response is, "Why don't you show the Lord what you **want** to do and then pray for his help in doing it?" People don't want to hear that, however. It puts too much responsibility on them. By "waiting" on "the Lord's timing" they can make God accountable for their shortcomings and failures. Well, guess what? That's not the way it works.

There is no scriptural endorsement of laziness or stupidity

or fear. God has given to human beings a free will, but God has commanded us to make wise choices and to redeem our time on earth. Sitting and waiting for God's perfect timing is a limp-wristed, weak-kneed approach to making the most of life, because the fact is that God's perfect timing is **now.**

When I read my Bible, I find it full of blaring bugles and shouts of "forward!"

—"Even though I walk through the valley of the shadow of death, I will fear no evil" (Psalm 23:4).

—"Allow no sleep to your eyes, no slumber to your eyelids" (Proverbs 6:4).

—" 'Be strong, all you people of the land,' declares the Lord, 'and work. For I am with you" (Haggai 2:4).

—"If a man will not work, he shall not eat" (2 Thessalonians 3:10).

Reading such verses convinces me that God does not intend for me to be his wind-up doll, an unthinking automaton that plods along in the direction it is faced until it runs into a wall or tumbles down the stairs. Instead, these verses admonish me to get moving on my own, to make a God-honoring plan and fulfill it and to show some creative independence and responsibility.

I know a person who lost his job as a youth pastor after a change in his church's pastorate. This man felt that God was using this loss of job situation to tell him he should become a senior pastor at a church of his own. So he sent out his resumé to a hundred churches. Most did not respond. Those who did told him that his credentials were not adequate. They felt that his three-year Bible school diploma should be upgraded by further study to a bachelor's, then master's degree in theology.

The man did not want to hear such suggestions because it would mean making sacrifices he didn't relish—night school, homework, financial commitments for tuition. Consequently he stubbornly said that God wanted him to have a church of his own, and he would sit and wait until God opened a door for him. He's been working at a minimum-wage job for several years now, still sending out resumés to churches, and still waiting. And no door has been miraculously opened for him.

Another person I knew lost his job as an announcer at a Christian radio station due to a conflict of management styles with the program director. He, too, thought that this job-loss situation could be an opportunity for him to better himself. He sought advice from me and from his father and from other Christian business persons.

He also began to read every book he could get his hands on related to business. In time, he borrowed money and started his own advertising firm. When that succeeded and he had repaid his loan, he borrowed again and this time bought a one-third interest in a rental property. When that also succeeded and he had repaid that loan, he hired an employee and started a telephone message repeater business. Today, he lives in a big new home on a shaded two-acre lot. He owns two cars and a van and all three of his children attend private schools. He's tremendously successful and he would humbly but honestly admit that to you.

Why the vast difference in outcomes between these two people? Both men are good Christians; both are the same age; both are married with three children; both have modest formal educations and limited job experience. Yet one person has wound up in a hand-to-mouth existence and the other has become a successful entrepreneur.

In this situation, was it logical (or theological, for that matter) to say that it was God's perfect timing in the first person's life that kept him from becoming a church pastor and from fulfilling his greatest ambition? I think not. The answer is far more obvious: **Free will gives a person the freedom to succeed and the freedom to fail. The choice is the individual's.**

Let that sink in on you. Ponder it long enough and you will realize it is true. God has given us self-autonomy with no strings attached. This gift of free will is so complete, that a person can even choose to scoff at the plan of salvation and die and spend an eternity in hell. Now that's a horrifyingly sober thought—but it's true nonetheless.

God expects us to justify our free will by finding ways to do good work. The Bible is filled with people who were active—not passive—heroes. They worked in a variety of ways—but they worked!

Noah **built** the ark.

David **fought** the giant.

Paul **debated** the Sanhedrin.

Moses **challenged** the pharaoh.

Daniel **entered** the lions' den.

Joshua **conquered** the Promised Land.

Solomon **constructed** the Holy Temple.

Peter **evangelized** the Greeks and Romans.

Jesus **preached, healed, taught, loved, and sacrificed.**

The intensity of time and mission is what has made great leaders fulfill their sense of personal destiny. Reflecting upon his past, Napoleon wrote, "Even when I had nothing to do, I vaguely knew I had no time to lose." Time has only stood still once in history and the Bible warns us that "there has never been a day like it before or since" (Joshua 10:14). Since that is the case, like Napoleon, we also have no time to lose.

If you have felt that you have been more guilty of rusting out than wearing out, that's good. I call that **creative discontent.** You're uneasy about the aimless way your life is drifting and you want to redirect your course. Good. I can help you. You don't have to become great at something overnight. In fact, it can't be done that way. But one step at a time will get you to where you want to be. So, let's start walking!

If You Lose Your Job, Don't Lose Your Head

Being dismissed from a job can be the worst and most traumatic form of rejection a person ever faces. If this happens to you, don't panic. Think clearly, exercise all your options, and direct yourself back into the work force. Here are some procedures to follow:

1. See if you can obtain a lump-sum payment from your pension plan upon leaving your employer.

2. Ask for your share of the company's profit-sharing plan if you were in such a program.

3. Find out if your union, professional association, or government program provides a "supplementary unemployment benefit" from a general employee's fund.

4. Request your severance pay, if applicable.

5. Contact your creditors by letter, explain your circumstances, and ask for reduced and extended or deferred payment plans.

6. Reduce family spending and see if other members of the family can find full- or part-time employment.

7. Register with several employment agencies and be aggressive in sending out resumes on your own.

8. Borrow against your permanent life insurance policies if a cash flow problem arises.

9. File for your state unemployment insurance benefits.

10. Use the Department of Labor's *Occupational Outlook Handbook* for career information and job-retraining programs.

Sample Planning Sheet

Life Priorities	Related Tasks
#1 CHURCH SERVICE	Drive church bus Help at Bible school Start a prayer group
#2 FAMILY RELATIONS	Teach Tommy to ride bike Lead nightly devotions Plan summer vacation
#3 CAREER ADVANCEMENT	Analyze the competition Explore new markets Finish college degree
#4 GOOD HEALTH	Lose ten pounds Increase stamina
#5 FINANCIAL SECURITY	Obtain adequate insurance Build retirement fund Reduce general spending Prepare for Christmas

for Life Directions

Time Frame	Anticipated Actions
Start route in May June 8 - 12 Sept. - Dec.	Apply for chauffeur's license Review curriculum materials Put sign-up sheet on bulletin board at church
Practice Each Evening Right After Supper July 18 - 24	Buy training wheels Ask pastor to suggest a book Rent cabin
During May May - Dec. 1989 - 1992	Read trade journals Attend seminars Visit new stores Travel Read Attend night school each Monday
Within 90 days Ongoing	Call doctor for approved diet Raquetball at noon, 3 Day/ week
During May Starting in July NOW! May - Nov.	Call agent for policy reviews Increase payroll contributions Eliminate four credit cards Open a Christmas account at bank

"Persistence Is the Common Denominator Among Highly Successful People."

Chapter 8:

Five Steps to Personal Freedom

I n this chapter we will look at specific steps that will take you closer to transforming creative discontent into genuine creativity that moves you forward toward your goals. Learning to make wise choices and implement them is crucial to your success.

Step #1: Define your priorities.

Sit down with a piece of paper and make a list of the things that are truly important to you: service to God; family life; financial security; job or career advancement; personal health; recreation; community service. Make the list as long as you wish. When you finish, go through and number each item according to the degree of its importance. Cross out any items that are repetitive or are really not all that important upon a second consideration.

Step #2: Assign tasks to each priority.

For each priority you listed in step one, list one or more specific things you could do to enhance that priority. For example, if one of your priorities is to do service to God, you may list next to it "join the church choir" and "volunteer to teach Sunday school." If another priority is job advancement, you may list "complete my college degree," "expand my sales territory," and "become the district manager." In each instance, move from general priorities to specific goals.

Step #3: Set time limits for each project.

Let nothing be abstract. Be as concrete and point blank as possible in all that you plan. Create time frames, deadlines, and project procedures. Note your goal completion dates next to each project. Make the deadlines realistic and reasonable, yet challenging. Keep in mind that you're playing catch-up ball.

Step #4: Anticipate problems and start solving them ahead of time.

Don't imagine that you won't be confronted by problems. You will be. Knowing in advance about possible pitfalls, however, will help you sidestep them. Try to come up with as many ideas and options as possible so that you'll never feel trapped. If one door closes, you can try another. For example, if you want to complete your college degree but the problem of finances worries you, you could list several options:

find an additional part-time or weekend job
borrow from your bank
use the G.I. Bill of Rights
establish a home-equity account
seek scholarships
file for federal aid to students
apply for college fellowships
pursue private grants
sell the lake cottage or second car
ask the spouse to find a job
borrow against some life insurance policies
enroll under a work-study program
use all savings
liquidate a rare coin or stamp collection
win a scholastic prize
ask to receive a future inheritance early
sublet the basement as an apartment

Here we have come up with seventeen solutions to one problem. It's hard to be caught off guard when you have so many ready options. Think and you will succeed.

Step #5: Put your plan into action.

Get started right away on completing the projects that will enhance your life priorities. Do something each day that will move you closer to reaching your ultimate goals—and remember our previous talk about persistence.

My Action Plan

1. _____

_____

_____

2. _____

_____

_____

3. _____

_____

_____

4. _____

_____

_____

5. _____

_____

"You can't build a reputation on what you're going to do."
—Henry Ford

Chapter 9:

Enthusiasm for Work

W alter Russell once noted, quite correctly, "Mediocrity is self-inflicted; genius is self-bestowed."

If you are to be a success at this "self-bestowing" of genius of which he speaks, it will be because of your ability to direct your career firmly toward successful ends. A person can do this in several ways. You can develop enthusiasm for work, learn to set worthy goals, know how to deal with temporary setbacks, formulate a personal continuing-education game plan, know when and if a complete career change may be warranted. These are some of the topics we will now focus on in this chapter.

Enthusiasm has been described in a variety of ways—drive, energy, inspiration, eagerness, excitement, ebullience, high spirits. Though hard to label with a single term, enthusiasm can best be summarized as **a direction of power stimulated by an individual's utter belief in something.** The more sold on something a person is, the more enthusiastic that person will be about it.

If all the members of a sales team are fairly equally matched with respect to experience and other factors, the one who will lead the team in sales will be the person with the most enthusiasm. The person with the worst sales record will be the person with the lowest level of enthusiasm for his or her work and career.

Ironically, sometimes the difference between the leader of

the pack and the "also-rans" is just a modest increase in enthusiasm. Sometimes it doesn't take much to change a situation. As noted motivational speaker Dr. Paul J. Meyer has observed, "The difference between water and steam is just one degree of temperature." A little bit more enthusiasm can sometimes make all the difference between one result or another.

How does one develop enthusiasm? For me it's not an instantaneous process when it comes to work. I usually build up steam for a project the more I become involved in it and the more I learn about it. Usually, enthusiasm is the end result of a four-phase process:

1. **The Question**—Any project has to begin with an element of wonder. Someone has to say, "I wonder what that's all about?" or "Hmmm, now there's something unusual; how can that be just so?"

2. **The Motivator**—After wondering about something, a person next has to have a reason for wanting to explore it further. The person has to think, If I were to master this new skill, I could gain a promotion or If I could understand more about these new computers, I could be more competitive in my field. There has to be some form of personal benefit related to the project before a person will consider pursuing it.

3. **The Research**—Having become convinced that it would be beneficial to become personally involved in this new project, the person next needs to build his confidence in regard to being able to handle the project. This comes through research. The process of reading, studying, and obtaining insights into the topic provides an educational foundation upon which the person can base his or her decisions and actions.

4. **The Goal**—With this understanding of why the project is worthwhile and how it can be handled, the only thing remaining for the person is to set a completion date for the project.

In the case of my work as a writer, quite often I am struck by an idea to explore in a new book (the **Question**). Some ideas I abandon as being shallow, boring, or frivolous; other times I get fired up about the opportunity to learn about a fascinating new subject (the **Motivator**). At that point I begin to learn all I can about the subject so that a year or so later I will be able to write about it (the **Research**). I then work out an outline for the book, set a date for its completion, secure a contract from my publisher, and get to work (the **Goal**). By the time my contract is signed, my enthusiasm is at a peak level.

Enthusiasm is needed for good work to be produced. Unfortunately, most of us have been conditioned over the years to quell our spontaneous enthusiasm and exuberance. As children we were told to sit still in church, to stop running in the school halls, not to speak out of turn, to quit squirming at the table. I am all in favor of manners and discipline. My caution to people is not to confuse the need for politeness with the dampening of enthusiasm. They are not the same.

Recent expounders of motivational theories, ranging from Leo Buscaglia to Jane Brody, have endorsed a little kicking up of the heels in order to maintain one's enthusiasm. Buscaglia tells people to run through the leaves in a park if the urge strikes them. Brody claims that one of the best ways to avoid burnout is to do something absolutely zany at least once a month. What can you do to cultivate enthusiasm?

❝In almost any subject, your passion for the subject will save you. If you care enough for a result, you will most certainly attain it. You must really wish this thing and wish it with exclusiveness, and not wish at the same time a hundred other incompatible things just as strongly.❞
—Dr. William James

Chapter 10:

Goalposts and Bull's-eyes

Prior to writing my book *Staying Ahead of Time*, I was unaware of the countless numbers of people who were leading utterly aimless lives. In that book on time management I introduced my readers to a planning grid I had developed called the "Life Map." Its function was to make people write down on paper what they wanted to accomplish within the next one-, three-, five-, fifteen-, and thirty-year time periods.

Another part of the "Life Map" called for a person to write down what her or his personal accomplishments to date had been and then to speculate about what her or his life-time accomplishments would be. This latter part was done by writing a make-believe obituary notice or *Who's Who* entry.

This goal-setting exercise proved to be a cold shower for many people. I have received stacks of letters from readers who have told me they had no direction in life until they made themselves sit down and fill in the "Life Map."

"It was a sobering experience," a 40-year-old salesperson wrote to me. "When I filled in my list of accomplishments, I had very little to show for four decades of living. I had always carried vague dreams of someday reaching some kind of recognized success. All I was doing, however, was getting through one day at a time. That was okay for a while. But now, for crying out loud, I'd hit forty. You made me see I had to stop clowning around and get serious about my life."

A homemaker in Iowa who had always "one day" hoped to become the owner of a florist shop wrote to me saying that if she had used the "Life Map" a decade earlier, she probably would now have been able to open a second florist shop. As it was, she still hadn't started the first one.

Goal setting is the only thing that will enable you to keep your life from slipping away before you can accomplish anything with it. The goal-oriented individual realizes that targets, goals, directions and priorities are the factors that map the path to success. Life is not a rehearsal. This is the real thing. Don't ad-lib your existence. Get it right.

Let's review some of the factors I consider to be essential for success-oriented goal setting:

- Goals **must** be written down and referred to on a regular basis.
- Goals should include spiritual, mental, physical, social, and financial advancements.
- Goals must be realistic, yet challenging.
- Goals must be supported by specific plans of action designed to help reach them.
- Goals must be reviewed, updated, and analyzed at set intervals.

A summary overview of goal setting can probably best be stated as this: **People usually get to where they plan to go.** If you make no plans, you do indeed arrive nowhere. If, however, you design very specific goals for yourself, lock those goals into a time frame, and then develop and institute action plans for achieving those goals, you become so laserlike in your focus that you cut through everything in getting to that goal.

Chapter 11:

Establishing Priorities in Goal Setting

A s you ponder about your aspirations, dreams, and ambitions for your life, you will quickly realize that you will need to accomplish your most important goals first. To discover what these goals are for your particular situation in life, respond on paper to each of these questions:

1. What weight should I be?

2. In what ways could my physical condition be improved?

3. When do I want to buy my next car? next home?

4. How much retirement income do I want to have saved by age sixty-five?

5. Where and when do I want my next vacation to be?

6. What social and civic activities would I enjoy joining?

7. When can I reduce my current debt load?

8. What sorts of business honors do I desire?

9. When will I begin to spend more time with my family?

10. What additional education do I need to obtain?

11. Which clients and prospects do I want to service more professionally?

12. When would I like to expand my business?

13. How much money do I want to earn this year?

14. Which old friendships would I like to rekindle?

15. When do I plan to review my total insurance coverage?

16. In what ways can I improve my wardrobe?

17. When will I have my will drawn up (or updated)?

18. How disciplined is my moral and religious life?

19. Which five books should I try to read very soon?

20. My greatest yet-unfulfilled life's ambition is what?

**"Success-oriented goalsetting
is a combination of establishing
security, taking regular but
feasible risks, and developing a
mental attitude that can cope with—
even expect—occasional setbacks."**

Chapter 12:

Coping with Setbacks

F or people who are new at goal setting, it can be very frustrating when unexpected interferences occur that delay or sidetrack an ongoing action plan. For some people a sudden cash flow drain, a canceled business deal, or the loss of an important client can be enough to send them into a severe depression. Sometimes their disappointment is so great that they abandon their goals altogether.

These people are not able to see setbacks as temporary situations. Indeed, for them, such setbacks may not be temporary. But that is only because they have not done the proper groundwork that will allow them to work confidently during both rough and smooth times.

What do I mean by groundwork? Simply this: you need to establish in advance a fixed security program for yourself and your dependents. Let me use myself as an example.

When I was a child I read Jules Verne's adventure novel *Around the World in Eighty Days*. The one thing that struck me about the main character, Phileas Fogg, was his preparedness. In any situation, he always had something to fall back on.

For example, when crossing from Europe to Africa, Fogg paid the steamship captain a bonus to deliver him to his port of call two days ahead of schedule. Later in the novel, when Fogg is told that a railway line is not open and he will have to take an elephant ride overland and thus waste two precious days, he does not panic. He smiles and says, "I figured something like this would happen. That's why I had the steamship captain help us gain two days a few weeks ago. So, we're still right on schedule. Let's go."

Fogg's clear-headedness and calm behavior were possible because he had a fail-safe system for everything. In my own life, I've established the same fail-safe system and because of it I always know that even if the bottom drops out of everything, I'll still be all right.

I own two homes, one large and one small. The smaller home is a rental property. Why? Because if worse ever comes to worst, I know I'll always have a place to live.

I have a garage closet filled with freeze-dried meats, nitrogen-packed fruits and vegetables, air-tight packages of soup, candy, vitamins and cereals, bottles of vinegar, cooking oil, and extra supplies of household articles, hygiene products, oil, kerosene, gasoline, and car parts. Why? Because if worse ever comes to worst, I'll still be able to feed my family and keep everyone warm for three months without outside help.

In my safe-deposit box I have a modest holding of U.S. savings bonds, silver dollars, and gold Kruggerrands. These are never touched. They just sit there. Why? Because if worse ever comes to worst, I'll always have some form of marketable securities by which I can raise emergency cash.

Am I a doom-sayer? a radical survivalist? an isolationist?

No, by no means. What I am is prepared.

Imagine what it does to you when you can go into contract negotiations, job interviews, or consulting discussions knowing that you can deal from strength; knowing, if I get this job, okay, but if I don't, there will be others; knowing, there's no need for knee scraping, head bowing, or customer worshiping. I'm not desperate.

Imagine how you can react when a hit from your blindside puts a real crimp in one of your plans to reach a goal. No problem. You're prepared. Like Phileas Fogg, you figured something was bound to go wrong, and so you set aside some extra cash and allowed for some extra time. This temporary setback can be dealt with and then things can be on their way again to reaching the goal.

The mistake that novice goal-setters make too often is in setting high and demanding goals for themselves that require them to stretch their finances and personal talents to dangerous limits. They string out their risks like lined-up dominoes. Things are precariously all right so long as no one sneezes. Let one domino start to fall, however, and in short order everything has toppled.

The wise goal-setter sets up five dominoes, builds a failsafe wall in front of them, and then sets up five more dominoes. As this process continues, the line of dominoes grows longer and longer (homes, cars, businesses, investments). From time to time the builder sneezes and the dominoes fall; but no more than five ever fall at once, and those five have no effect on the previously erected well-fortified line of other dominoes.

Success-oriented goal setting is a combination of establishing security, taking regular but feasible risks, and developing a mental attitude that can cope with—even expect—occasional setbacks.

⚞⚟⚞⚟⚞⚟⚞⚟⚞⚟⚞⚟⚞⚟⚞⚟⚞⚟⚞⚟⚞⚟⚞⚟⚞⚟⚞⚟⚞⚟⚞⚟⚞⚟

**_"_A man who would
move the world
must first
move himself._"_
—Socrates**

⚞⚟⚞⚟⚞⚟⚞⚟⚞⚟⚞⚟⚞⚟⚞⚟⚞⚟⚞⚟⚞⚟⚞⚟⚞⚟⚞⚟⚞⚟⚞⚟⚞⚟

Chapter 13:

Career Changes

I n my seminars on time management and goal setting, a question invariably arises concerning whether or not a person should make a complete career change. For example, a forty-six-year-old factory supervisor asked me, "What do you think I should do? I want to be a millionaire by the time I'm seventy, but my job in the factory has me locked in at $39,000 a year. How can my goals match my circumstances?"

The simple answer is that **circumstances have to be arranged so that goals can be achieved, and not the other way around.** Quite often this means having to leave a deadend career in order to start over in something with more potential. But, at other times, it can mean staying in the same career and either you must lower outrageous expectations or else discover new ways to gain advancement within the current career.

The first step in deciding whether or not a career change is the right move is to assess what all your current job is providing you:

Continuing Education Programs?
Paid Vacations?
Sales Competition Prizes?
Life Insurance?
Flex-Time Work Schedule?

Company Product Discounts?

Profit-Sharing Plan?

Stock Options?

Retirement Plans?

Company Trips?

Disability Insurance?

Company Car?

Expense Account?

Christmas Bonus?

Dental Plan?

Commissions?

If you put a dollar amount on each of your fringe benefits, you might discover that the $5,000 raise a new job offers really isn't worth the $6,300 worth of benefits you would forfeit leaving the present job.

You next must compare your dollar amount raises each year to the rise in inflation. In a roller-coaster economy like ours, which had inflation at nearly 14 percent from 1980 to 1982, then down to 3 percent from 1983 to 1988, you can often be fooled by your supposed buying power. Obtain a free copy of the *Consumer Price Index* by calling the Bureau of Labor at (202) 272-5160 and then check the percentage of your raises with the percentage of inflation. If you've been losing buying power each year, it may be time to get into a more financially lucrative career.

Your third step is to decide what kind of career change you feel would suit you best. Explore several options:

1. **Radical change**—a completely new career in a different company or entry into self-employment.
2. **Lateral change**—same job but for a different employer.
3. **Internal change**—a new job but for your current employer.
4. **Directional change**—staying in the same general field but specializing in a new area (management instead of customer service; municipal auditing instead of general accounting).

Before closing any career doors, you would be wise to explore all your career options that these four choices suggest.

Your next step will be to decide when you would best be ready to make a career change. Do you need to brush up on certain skills first? Do you need to spend a few months catching up on all the current trade journals in that field? Do you want to complete a project for your current employer so that you can leave on good terms? Set a specific target date and gear toward it.

Your final step will be to devise a plan by which you can gain access to a new career field. Here are several suggestions:

Employment agencies.

Ads in trade journals.

Want ads in newspapers.

Direct contact with company executives.

Mass mailings of your resume.

Visits to businesses to fill out applications.

Notifying friends that you are looking for new work.

If upon analyzing all the pro and con aspects of changing careers you are convinced that it is the only way for you to advance yourself and to reach the goals you feel you need to be striving for, then do it. Have serious talks with your spouse and dependents; seek their input and then move ahead without looking back.

If, on the other hand, you should decide that a career change would be too risky or not worth the effort financially or for other reasons, your best alternative would be to stay in your current career, but initiate an aggressive personal continuing-education program so that you can stay current and competitive in your field.

**"As a man thinketh
in his heart,
so is he."**
—King Solomon

Chapter 14:

Continuing Education

C areer momentum for the motivated Christian is maintained through continuous study. You must always be looking for new topics, new trends, new developments, new techniques, and new ideas to study and master so that you can remain productive. The more you know, the more you will be able to do for God, your family, and yourself.

There will never come a time in your personal career in which you will be able to say, I now know enough. This is because even if you are able to become an expert on virtually every aspect of the career in which you are involved, you will still be responsible for the overall nurturing and development of the people. And that requires diversity.

Because of this, your professional interests must be broadly based. Not only do you need to spend time learning more about your own career and its many diverse elements, but also to be a student of public relations, sales, financing, leadership, public speaking, time management, and communication. New books on these subjects and articles in trade periodicals should be the core of your ongoing personal reading program.

You would do well to hone your list of subscriptions to trade periodicals so that you receive primarily those magazines and newsletters that relate closest to your work. As you read these publications, get into the habit of tearing out useful articles and filing them for future reference. If you find something of solid value to everyone in your office or church or Bible study group, put a "buck slip" on it and circulate it. Highlight key passages with yellow felt-tip highlighting marking pens.

How to Be Innovative

Evaluate the opportunities for change, modification, enhancement, remodeling, and restructuring in all the systems and products that are already working well for you.

Analyze the way people use your product or service. Ask them what they hate about it and eliminate that; ask them what they like about it and enhance that. Continue to make things easier and easier to understand and use.

Experiment with a few radical changes, but test-market them in a limited area to be sure they are acceptable. Study businesses totally unrelated to yours to see what ideas you can borrow and adapt for your line of work. Keep a product or service exactly the way it is, but market it a whole new way.

Chapter 15:

Directed Study

In order to maximize your self-training, you should take time to think about the future. Ask yourself some fundamental questions:

What new problems will my career need to respond to in the coming years?

What projects does my manager or partner plan to initiate in the next one to five years?

Which areas of professional development do I need to improve on in the near future?

How can I help improve the perception of my job, my business office, my company, and my industry as a whole in the next few years?

If you are not sure of the answers to these questions, seek your answers. Make notes and records of what you discover. Organize your thoughts. Take time to lay out a careful plan of study for yourself. Include seminars and workshops as part of your training, not just for the knowledge being shared but also for the opportunity to observe firsthand how the trainers and lecturers are presenting material to their audiences. Night school at a local college or correspondence courses also are good ways to expand your knowledge.

Here are some suggestions on how to make your self-study efforts most effective as they integrate with the Life Directions ideas we looked at earlier:

1. Establish long-range objectives. Just knowing where you are going will get you there faster. So, prepare a list of specific objectives that you feel would benefit your career once reached. Attach a time limitation to each goal so that you will feel a sense of urgency about completing it. For example, write, "Complete the MBA diploma course during the next twenty-four months" or "Read one business book per month this year." Try to forecast your professional growth needs at least five years into the future.

2. Set priorities. If you work sincerely at analyzing your career development needs for the next five years, you will have a considerable list of topics to explore. Don't try to juggle a dozen of these activities simultaneously; instead, set your list in priority order according to those things that will help you grow to your full career potential or will expand and nurture the talents of your fellow Christians. Set target goals, complete each level, and direct all your concentration on the important priorities. Master one new area of knowledge well, then move on.

3. Upgrade your performance standards. To prevent yourself from becoming complacent and satisfied with your educational progress, learn to demand more of yourself with each new year of experience gained.

4. Assume new responsibilities. Even if you have a specific job description that somewhat limits your focus and direction, you will never be limited on how far you can go within the realm of that job description. Study new skills, keep current on all career-related news, and assist others in the overall mission. You will gradually be called upon to assume more and more responsibilities. You will be called upon to manage a variety of new matters. The more knowledgeable and diversified you are, the more responsibilities you will be capable of accepting.

Summary

In Part 4 we have examined how enthusiasm as a four-stage process can be self-generated for work-related projects. We also saw how and explained why success-oriented goal setting is a necessary aspect of the overall motivational process. With that, we noted that unless an individual has secured a fail-safe backup security plan for his or her risks, the goal-setting process will not work. We concluded by outlining the ways to determine whether one should seek his or her goals by changing careers or by advancing one's self through continuing education in the career at hand. Through it all we discovered that goal setting is a serious and challenging, but highly worthwhile, aspect of personal success.

Part 5:

Physical, Emotional, and Spiritual Harmony

A ll your life you've heard the clichés, jingles, limericks and one-liners about good health:

"Early to bed, early to rise, makes a man healthy, wealthy, and wise."

"When you've got your health, you've got just about everything."

"Strong body, strong mind."

"Take care of your body and your body will take care of you."

"An apple a day keeps the doctor away."

The interesting observation is that a saying has to be around a long time and used a great deal before it actually becomes a cliché. Often the way it can stay around a long while is because there's some truth to it; hence, the abundance of clichés about the necessity of good health as a priority to success. They do have a great deal of validity to them.

My purpose here will not be to provide a regimen of diet, exercise, and sleep programs for you to follow. Instead, I simply wish to underscore that unless you keep your body in adequate condition, you will be physically unable to be up for battle.

Fortunately, common sense and some basic understanding of physical maintenance can go a long way in helping you maintain the stamina and strength needed for career success. The body is a resilient and durable biochemical apparatus, but like any functioning mechanism it needs proper care if its durability is to last. In Part 5, let's review some of the basic ways in which you may maximize the use of your body while also meeting its needs.

Chapter 16:

Sleep and Exercise

How Much Sleep?

According to recent research conducted by the Association of Sleep Disorders Center (P.O. Box YY, East Setauket, NY 11733), people vary widely in their sleep needs. Some people can function perfectly on four hours' sleep per day, whereas, conversely, a newborn infant usually sleeps twenty hours per day.

Medical advice used to recommend eight hours of uninterrupted sleep per day; ironically, most physicians making these recommendations were existing quite well on four to seven hours of catch-as-catch-can sleep.

In extensive research that I did when writing my book *Positive Workaholism*, I discovered that **no** highly successful business leader was in the habit of sleeping eight or more hours consecutively each day. Furthermore, very few of them felt compelled to sleep at normally accepted sleeping hours, either.

The discoveries were personally **very comforting** to me in that I probably have one of the **more bizarre** sleep patterns you might ever hear about. I **really enjoy** the solitude and quietude of nights. As a writer, I find I am most productive between 10 P.M. and 4 A.M. The phone isn't ringing, the TV is off, the kids are in bed, and no one is **banging on my door** trying to sell me candy or magazine subscriptions. I can work uninterrupted, and I covet this temporary Trappist life each night.

I find that if I get four or five hours of sleep between 4 A.M. and 9 A.M. and then take a nap after dinner, my energy levels stay high.

Sensible, Effective Exercise

The 1980s found many Americans obsessed with a fitness fetish. In 1983 Americans spent $5.2 billion on health club activities, $1.1 billion on jogging footwear, and nearly $2 billion on medical bills related to injuries that occurred while engaging in conditioning activities.

That tells us something. Namely, that a great many people are willing to spend a lot of money and willing to risk a great deal of pain just to get fit quickly. As the medical bills indicate, that isn't the answer. Sensible, regular, appropriate exercise programs should be sought by rational people. There are no overnight remedies.

Exercise programs are important for the business person who wishes to increase her or his level of motivation. People who are physically fit enjoy greater longevity, better daily health, more strength by which to tackle work, and noticeably increased productivity.

Coaches and authorities on sports medicine say that total conditioning calls for a blend of exercises and sports activities. They recommend the following areas of emphasis:

Hand-to-eye-coordination development—volleyball, handball, tennis or table tennis, and golf.

Stamina and respiratory development—aerobic workouts, skipping rope, long-distance running, and vigorous swimming.

Coordination and balance development—warm-up stretching, ballet, gymnastics, and calisthenics.

Muscle building—weight-lifting, push-ups and pull-ups, isometrics, punching-bag workouts, and rowing.

Simple exercises such as sit-ups, push-ups, jogging in place, jumping rope, and isometrics can be done at no investment in equipment or clothing gear and can be engaged in at home or in a hotel room when away on business. Naturally, it is wise to consult your family physician for a physical examination before engaging in any new exercise program.

"Since we each get just
one today, it makes sense
to take good care of it.**"**

Chapter 17:

Food Choices

A machine is only as efficient as the fuel it runs on. For the person who desires to remain motivated, good nutritional eating habits are a must. In truth, most of us are poor judges of which foods are best for us, which quantities are most beneficial, and what times of day are best for eating. A little enlightenment on some of these areas should prove helpful.

Breakfast is an important meal. It's good to make it the most substantial meal of the day. Lunch and dinner could be a bit lighter. Few Americans are in this habit, but those who are have shown measurable increases in performance.

Snacking on the job can be a negative factor in motivation. For example, if a person takes a break and grabs a cup of coffee and a jelly donut, the quick boost of energy generated from the donut's sugar will only last twelve to sixteen minutes. Thereafter, the body will release natural insulin to cope with the sugar. The result is a major **drop** of the blood-sugar level that, in turn, causes yawning, new hunger pangs, fatigue, and irritability. It's not worth it. Consider leaving even a ten-calorie serving of refined sugars and flours out of your diet before lunch—or better yet—altogether.

Balancing a diet is the key objective in all eating habits. If the body ingests too much refined sugar, it will not ingest enough nutrients. If the body takes in too much protein, the chemicals of the blood will become distorted and this will put stress on the kidneys. Too much cholesterol will clog the blood vessels. About the only food unit without a danger potential is the complex carbohydrate group.

Salt intake should also be limited. People need only one gram of salt per day (a scant ½ teaspoon altogether) and since most processed foods contain one or two percent salt anyway, most people are already getting far more salt than needed each day.

Natural foods containing no dyes or preservatives should be part of a balanced diet. A 1977 survey by scientists showed that the average American ate 5½ pounds of needless food chemicals annually. That's 358 pounds of chemicals flushed through your system from birth to age 65. Common sense will tell you that that can't be a positive situation.

The body contains 100 trillion cells. The average adult male needs about 2,500 to 2,900 calories per day to operate this complex unit. Ingesting more than this can lead to obesity. At present, approximately 35 percent of all Americans are obese and another 22 percent are heavier than their recommended weight.

Obesity (20 percent or more over ideal weight) is certainly to be avoided by the enthusiastic Christian. According to 1975 statistics compiled by Metropolitan Life Insurance Company, men who are 10 percent overweight increase their likelihood of premature death by 13 percent, those 20 percent overweight a 25 percent chance, and men who are 30 percent overweight a 43 percent chance of early death. In short, lean is keen, but fat is foolish.

Fad diets can be very dangerous. A few years ago an all-liquid protein diet became very popular. Somehow the conclusion was reached that, since proteins are used to form antibodies, protein was its own form of protection, and, since protein was more easily digested than fat, it would keep people lean.

It didn't work that way, however. Some people actually died as a result of that diet. It had two major flaws: first, extra protein (or extra **anything**) goes into Kreb's Cycle in the body and gets converted to body fat, and second, the body needs a variety of some forty nutrients, fats, carbohydrates, and proteins in order to survive. Therefore, all diets should first be sanctioned by your physician or nutritionist.

Vitamin fads are also to be cautioned against. Not long ago, vitamin E was being touted as a cure for everything from infertility to cancer. In truth, vitamin E is primarily a natural preservative that retards oxygen from destroying vitamin A and other substances.

Here are basic rules of thumb:

1. Since vitamin C and B vitamins are water soluable, they must be replaced in the system daily.
2. The body has a limited ability to absorb iron, and so it should be part of a daily diet.
3. Minerals and trace minerals make up four percent of the body's weight and, though small, they must be supplied on a regular basis to avoid goiter, tooth decay, and stunted growth.

Since we each get just one body, it makes sense to take good care of it. The Bible also reminds us that our bodies are the temples of the Lord. Oddly enough, the very person who would never dream of spray-painting obscenities on the walls of a church might very easily be someone who has allowed himself or herself to become grossly overweight or has developed a habit of smoking or has never bothered to eat a balanced diet. As a result, she or he has defaced and damaged the temple of the Lord. Paul wrote in Romans 12:1, "Therefore, I urge you, brothers, in view of God's mercy to offer your bodies as living sacrifices, holy and pleasing to God—this is your spiritual act of worship."

John the Baptist lived on honey and locusts. Daniel existed ten days on water and pulse (salad greens) rather than touch the meat sacrificed to pagan gods. God-honoring people have shown how to be "living sacrifices" many times in the Scriptures. In doing your "spiritual worship" you, too, should keep your personal temple in good condition. I once heard a sports announcer comment on the irony of professional football: it is a game in which "a stadium filled with 78,000 people in need of exercise watch 22 men in need of rest."

I trust that you will be a participant rather than an observer.

Chapter 18:

Emotional Tie-ins

The close relationship between the physical and emotional well-being of a person is so direct that physicians believe more than half of their patients who complain of physical exhaustion are actually suffering from emotional stress. In the majority of instances, the stress is manifested as a result of boredom, worry, or fear of failure. This leads to insomnia, tension, headaches, and all-around fatigue. Let's examine these three emotional problems.

Boredom is frequent among people who have repetitious jobs or predictable days. They need challenges, physical and mental stimulation, new experiences. I recall that when I was in basic training during my hitch in the army, we used to take hikes from five- to twenty-miles long. The hikes may have helped to condition me physically, but they bored me mentally. I used to deal with this situation by composing long letters in my head to my parents, girl friend, brother, and friends. I would make up humorous stories, categorize our training activities, describe the military base in great detail, and compile a long list of items I needed sent to me.

At the end of the day when we would return to our barracks and have some free time before lights out, I would actually put these letters on paper and get them ready to mail. This sort of disciplined daydreaming, I'm convinced, helped me keep my sanity.

Combating boredom is something the industrial world has had to deal with, too. Assembly line workers at automobile plants were resorting to the use of illegal drugs to help them cope with the tediousness of spending eight hours per day for twenty years putting Part A into Slot B. Their subsequent lack of quality control and reduced efficiency led to substandard workmanship and poor products. Today in most production plants workers are rotated to a different job every six weeks in order to offer them some variety and challenge. This has resulted in better work and happier workers.

I can remember many days when the boredom of my job as a college public relations executive would make me exhausted by the end of the day. The job was not physically demanding at all, but the repetition of the work could numb the mind. For example, on one particular day I had to update the alumni information files. I spent eight hours pulling data cards and adding dull facts to them such as the names and birthdays of new children and the names of the latest clubs and organizations the individuals had joined.

When I came home that night I felt as if an anvil were perched on my shoulders. I told my wife that all I wanted to do was have a quick bite of supper and then collapse on the couch for a long nap. I couldn't remember ever having felt so tired.

Then, midway through our meal, the telephone rang. It was our pastor. He told me that several buddies of mine were back in town and they were visiting with him at the church.

"Terry Glidden and John Spring and Kevin Kotke all dropped in," he explained. "We put the volleyball net up and we're calling some folks to see if they'd like to come out to the church for a few sets. Do you and Rose want to join us?"

"Sure!" I responded enthusiastically. "We'll be there in fifteen minutes. I can't wait to see those guys."

I hung up the phone and relayed the news to my wife. She looked at me with a perplexed stare. "But ten minutes ago you were so tired you said you could barely walk," she reminded me. "And now you want to go play volleyball?"

"Of course!" I said. "Then was then. Now is now. Eat up and let's go."

One simple phone call had revitalized my whole system. My previous exhaustion had been caused by the boredom of my job that day. The sudden injection of a chance for fun, frolic, and fellowship shifted my mind off those boring things and redirected my thoughts to experiences that would buoy me up. With an enthusiastic mind, I gained an enthusiastic body.

I often remember that scene whenever I start to feel exhausted because of boredom. I take a break from what I am doing and read something uplifting, such as Psalm 96:

> Sing to the Lord a new song;
> > sing unto the Lord, all the earth.
> Sing to the Lord, praise his name;
> > proclaim his salvation day after day.
> Declare his glory among the nations,
> > his marvelous deeds among all peoples.
> For great is the Lord and most worthy of praise;
> > he is to be feared above all gods (vv. 1-4).

Keep in mind that the attitude you bring to your work makes a great deal of difference about whether the work will be boring or not. Mark Twain demonstrated this point in the famous fence-painting episode in *Tom Sawyer*. Most kids would have considered whitewashing a fence to be a boring and laborious job, but Tom pretended that he was having the time of his life while doing it. He was so convincing at feigning his merriment that the neighborhood youngsters asked Tom if he would let them try it, too.

Well, Tom wasn't about to forfeit his fun for nothing, but he said he would agree to make a swap or accept a payment. Soon, the area children were giving Tom an apple, a whistle, and other prize possessions in exchange for a chance to paint some of Aunt Polly's weatherbeaten old fence. Tom wound up with a pocketful of toys and the fence got painted with no effort on his part.

In the delightful children's story *Mary Poppins*, the ingenious Mary shows the children that even cleaning a room can be fun if you make a game of it. It's the spoonful of sugar—the challenge to make a game out of every chore—that helps the medicine go down, she explains.

An old Chinese legend makes the same point. An aging father had created a beautiful orchard during his lifetime, but his three lazy sons would not work in the orchard to maintain it. One day the father told the boys a secret: buried in the orchard was a great treasure. If the boys found it and dug it up, they could keep it. With visions of wealth and splendor before them, the three boys began to dig trenches between the rows of trees, searching for the treasure.

When the seasons changed and the rains filled the trenches, they served as irrigation ditches. This made the trees healthier than ever before and they bore an abundance of fruit that year. Seeing this, the old Chinese father said to his sons, "Congratulations. You have found the treasure."

Changing your attitude about your work is just one way to overcome boredom. Here are some other suggestions:

1. Drive to work a different way each day.
2. Develop a hobby that's very different from your job.
3. Plan a vacation out of state.
4. Develop new friendships.
5. Join a Bible study group.
6. Call a friend you haven't visited with in a long time.
7. Assist with a community service project.
8. Read entertaining novels.

The ironic fact about the fatigue caused by boredom is that it must be cured by activity and not by rest. So break out of the doldrums and you will have more energy.

Worry can be real or imagined. Either way, it wears you down. I know a person who will create something to worry about if there are no real problems at present. She will invite people to her house for a holiday dinner and then spend weeks agonizing over whether there will be enough food, whether everyone will make it home if it should snow, whether she's remembered to invite everyone who should be invited—just anything and everything. By the time the day finally arrives, she's a bundle of nerves. She runs around from room to room checking and rechecking everything to make sure it's all right, totally exhausting herself. She doesn't enjoy the day, she usually gets into a quarrel with her husband, and when it's all over she immediately begins to worry about how everything will ever get cleaned up again. It drives me crazy to be around on days like that.

I know another person whose worries are so systemized, she even preprograms her exhaustion and recovery periods. She will say, "We're leaving for Lake Tahoe on Friday and we'll be busy for five days. When we get back I'll need two days to catch up with my rest, and so I've canceled all my appointments in advance for those two days." This never ceases to amaze me. The anxiety she generates over a "pleasure trip" literally puts her flat on her back once it's over. To me, there's no point in taking the trip if it's going to cause more stress than relaxation. Besides, who says the trip won't invigorate rather than enhaust her? (**She** says it. By preprogramming the anticipated exhaustion, it never fails to generate itself.)

In Romans 8:28 we are told that "in all things God works for the good of those who love him." This is because Christians have a standard by which to fix their life's course. This standard is like a magnet that will pull them toward the good.

Think for a moment about how a steamship travels from Honolulu to San Francisco. The best route is a straight line from one port to the other. This is impossible to follow, however, because the ship is constantly being pulled off course by cross-currents or by strong winds. As this happens, the navigator checks the compass and steers the ship back on course. In time, its zigzag course brings the ship safely to its destination.

The Christian life this side of heaven works in a similar fashion. As people who know God's Word and understand it to represent the ultimate good in life, we work together to attain this goodness. Frequently, the challenges of life will knock us off course temporarily, but by checking the Bible (our compass) we can bring ourselves back toward the goodness. Often God can work toward achieving the good work we desire to do—even if some of the "things" are great hardships.

When John Bunyon was imprisoned for preaching the gospel, he used the years of solitude to write the great epic *Pilgrim's Progress*. When John Milton went blind, he used his inner sight to compose the moving passages in *Paradise Lost*. God can work in all things for good.

To defeat worry, I always tell people to use logic and faith. Is it logical to sit and wring your hands, worrying about failing a driver's test? No! It is logical to stay calm, perform the way you've been trained, show your skills, and pass the test. Whenever my young daughter Jeanette starts to worry and cry about a lost doll, a bad grade, a school paper, or a television show that she has missed, I always say to her, "Don't cry; think!" Once she stops crying and sits down and thinks things through, she realizes that one bad grade won't hamper her semester grade that much or one missed TV show in winter can be seen on summer reruns. The problem is that, being a child, she sometimes responds, "I don't want to think, daddy. I'm upset and I just want to cry." So, I let her.

Adults are like that sometimes, too. And, actually, that's not all bad. Some people can cry and release pent-up tension and then feel better. Only when the crying goes on unabated or occurs constantly or it does not subsequently lead to rational behavior do problems arise. An immature adult who refuses to confront his or her worries and deal with them is compounding the reasons **for** worry. A bad situation becomes worse.

If logic fails you, rely all the more on your faith. Take time to read passages of Scripture that will reassure you of God's love and protection. Share your worries with family members or close friends and draw strength from them. Don't worry— you're not alone.

Fear of failure can lead to a sense of depression that can physically drain a person. It makes us want to give up, roll into a ball, and die. I, personally, know what that is like. Because of retirements, moves, and other reasons, the chairperson of my doctoral committee was changed three times. Each change was a highly traumatic circumstance for me because each new person wanted to redirect my dissertation in a whole new way. Of course, I was powerless to prevent this, and so I had to live with my frustrations.

My first chairperson was a stickler for dates, direct quotations, multi-reference documents, and literary analysis. I worked nearly two years to write a dissertation that met his rigid standards. Before I had finished all the work, however, he resigned, and I was given a new chairperson who wanted the dissertation rewritten to reflect a more modern approach to literary research, namely a more readable style of writing. I started all over.

More than a year later I was almost finished with the revised version of my dissertation. My new chairperson called me one day and announced that he was going to retire six months earlier than he had originally planned. He sold his home in Indiana, moved to Florida, and I found myself with yet another chairperson. With great trepidation I sent both versions of the dissertation to the him. I asked if he would accept either one and allow me to convene my committee for a dissertation defense so that I could complete my doctor's degree.

After three weeks of nerve-wrecking waiting, I received a written response. The new chairperson didn't like the approach of either of the two dissertations I had written. He preferred a dissertation that was one-third biographical references, one-third literary criticism, and one-third new research. He instructed me to start over and to report to him after a year to discuss my progress.

I set the letter down, went into my bedroom, crawled into my bed, and pulled the covers over my head. I just wanted to stay hidden for the rest of my life. I wanted the Lord's return to come right then. I wanted to prick my finger on a spinning wheel and fall into a mindless trance or to go into the Catskills with Rip Van Winkle and fall asleep for twenty years. I wished I could take a nap and wake up to find out I'd only been having a nightmare. I hoped that my wife would come rushing upstairs yelling, "Look on the back of the letter, Dennis. It says, 'April Fool.' "

I wanted **anything** other than the situation I was faced with. I felt gutted, defeated, whipped, steamrolled, scoffed, mocked, bent, torn, spindled, and mutilated. This time the phoenix would not rise from its ashes. This time Rocky Balboa would not respond to the gong. There would be no late inning rally, no final jump shot, no last minute pass play. It was over. I was dead and I wanted to stay dead.

Fortunately, my dear wife had just the right words at a time like this to help me cope with this tragic ordeal. She came into our room, gently pulled down the covers and whispered to me, "Darling, I know you feel like you want to give up. But, sweetheart, I've been living like a pauper for the last four years so that we can get you through this program. So, you either get up out of that bed and go back to your writing desk on your own power or I'll be back in five minutes with a bucket of ice water. I don't mind struggling, but there has to be a pay-off."

Knowing that she wasn't bluffing, I got out of bed, took a deep breath, kicked the wall as hard as I could, and then went back to work. One year later I graduated with a doctor of philosophy degree in English from Ball State University and was named the "Distinguished Doctoral Graduate in English" that year. Had it not been for Rose, my overwhelming fear of failure might have kept me too mentally, physically, and emotionally drained to try again. (By the way, I dedicated my dissertation to my wife. Appropriate, eh?)

When you find yourself similarly confronted with what appears to be a task you can never accomplish, cut it down to size. Break the big job down into smaller little jobs. Finish them one at a time. No one could swallow a huge sausage and eat it without choking. Cut it into small slices, however, and you can eat the whole sausage a bit at a time.

Just remember: "Don't cry. Think!"

Factors of Poor Decision Making

Inefficiency—The person is incompetent and knows it. Thus he or she will try to delay confronting the issue or try to make it appear less important than it is or simply avoid the issue entirely.

Fear—The person is terrified of being held accountable for the actions and results of her decisions. Or he will stall for action until he can muster group support for the final choice.

Stupidity—The person always responds with gut instinct rather than doing careful research; as such, most decisions made are haphazard and harmful.

Seclusion—The person is capable of making adequate decisions but she is never around when you need her; she may be at another work site, off negotiating an overseas deal, or away on yet another vacation and cannot help you with your problem.

Disorganization—The person forgets meetings, doesn't respond to letters, loses memos, and misses deadlines. Hence, his decisions (good or bad) have no immediate value to anyone.

Diplomacy—The person knows what the correct decisions should be, but she will never vote against her superiors or argue with anyone who may be abe to help her up the success ladder later on. She says yes to everything.

Vacillation—The person makes a decision but later can be talked into reversing it if enough people criticize him; therefore, people cannot trust his decisions or act on them.

How to Make Wise Decisions

1. Invoke the counsel and guidance of the Holy Spirit through regular prayer.

2. Define your objectives in specific terms. Write them down and when in doubt refer to them. Keep on track.

3. Analyze all the variables. Before making a final decision, determine what the reaction or response to it will be from colleagues, competitors, and customers.

4. Gather data from trustworthy sources. Don't accumulate a lot of data—just the best data. Base your decision on solid facts, reliable experience, and unbiased views.

5. Devise a stand-by plan so that if your decision is wrong, you still have a backup system and there will be no need to panic.

Chapter 19:

Spiritual Strength

A few years ago an interviewer asked me if I was a secular writer or a Christian writer. I considered that a while before responding.

"I am a Christian who writes for a living," I answered at last. "Some of my articles appear in the secular newspapers and magazines, and some of my articles appear in religious and denominational publications. All my writing, however, reflects my Christian values and disciplines."

What the interviewer had meant by the question was, Where do I submit my articles to be published: secular or Christian periodicals? My answer expanded the question. I wanted the interviewer to understand that no matter what line of work a Christian is in, he or she carries his or her beliefs into the workplace. A Christian carpenter builds churches and Bible colleges, but he or she also builds office complexes and homes. There is no procedure for changing from Christian carpentry to secular carpentry. It's all one form of work—high quality performed "unto the Lord."

Non-Christians experience difficulty in understanding why we Christians are so different in our walk and talk and behavior.

Life deals us the same amount of challenges as unbelievers (Matthew 5:45 tells us that rain falls "on the just and unjust"), yet we seem to be able to handle things better emotionally and physically. "What makes you so different?" they want to know. Of course, the answer is the strength we draw from the indwelling Holy Spirit, but this sort of mystic response seems hard for nonbelievers to comprehend.

But it has always been that way. While the Egyptians were being plagued by sores, pestilence, and disease, God's people were unscathed by it all. The Scriptures tell us why in Exodus 15:26: "If you listen carefully to the voice of the Lord your God and do what is right in his eyes, if you pay attention to his commands and keep all his decrees, I will not bring on you any of the diseases I brought on the Egyptians, for I am the Lord, who heals you."

Nonbelievers do not understand that real success in life means harmony among mind, body, and soul. When these are synchronized, the result is joy.

Some philosophies call for the individuals to do their own thing. The watch phrase is, If it feels good, do it. Unfortunately, these are shallow options for people. They provide no lasting satisfaction. Instead, the "whole head is injured and [the] whole heart afflicted" (Isaiah 1:5). Humans need more. They need spiritual nurturing.

Unsaved people try to stimulate themselves with pills, powders, tobacco, whiskey, beer, and narcotics. Saved people present their bodies as living sacrifices.

Christians are not naive about life. Actually, they are better prepared—or should be—than anyone else. They can deal with any problem. First Corinthians 10:13 promises that no temptation will come to you except what is common to the human race. God is faithful and will not let you be tempted beyond your strength. When temptations come, God will also provide a way out so that you can stand up under them.

The whole purpose of this book has been to offer you insights on how you can be better prepared to maximize your life. God created men and women for divine fellowship. We have been given complete free will so that this could be genuine communion and not an artificial circumstance in which we obeyed directives out of fear rather than love. God also gave us the Bible as a textbook for life and encouraged us to help one another.

If reading this book has helped you, I'll feel pleased. But now it's your turn to use what you've learned here to help others. Do your work to the glory of God and it will always be something positive.

Habits of Great Leaders

- Great leaders **create** long-range **strategic** business **plans.**

- Great leaders **revise goals upward** on a regular basis.

- Great leaders **improve constantly** on **communication** skills.

- Great leaders **venture** into areas of **acceptable risk.**

- Great leaders **learn** by self-analysis and feedback from others.

- Great leaders **maintain** a position of **control** in matters.

- Great leaders **develop** ever **higher** levels of **self-confidence.**

- Great leaders **utilize** mental rehearsal techniques to **prepare for** speeches, meetings, or business **presentations.**

"Boredom and routine are two different things. It would be terrible to be bored, but it is essential to have a great deal of routine that allows you to do your work."
—Henry Moore,
Scupltor

Varieties of Learning Methods

Action Assignments: A specific skill or knowledge is applied to a real life situation on the job.

Automatic Instruction: Cassette tapes or video discs or workbooks are used to teach material presented in a programmed format.

Case Studies: A sales or marketing situation or product need is exemplified through the use of a hypothetical case history involving as many of the variables or properties of the subject in question as possible.

Coaching: A seasoned worker provides regular one-on-one coaching and counseling for a specific trainee.

Conference: A committee or team of workers meets together to develop group solutions to problems.

Demonstrations: An expert in some area explains and demonstrates how a particular process is handled.

Drill: A specific procedure is repeated until it is mastered.

Exposition: A lecturer or teacher uses charts, graphs, photos, displays, and samples to expound on how a particular procedure is to be followed.

Lectures: A prepared speech delivered by a teacher to an audience with time following for questions.

Peer Instruction: More experienced employees teach and coach a trainee under the buddy system.

Quizzes: Written or oral testing situation in which the student is required to explain memorized material, procedures learned, and policies understood.

Role Playing: Simulated job-related situations acted out by student and teacher to simulate job-related situations and help the trainee learn to anticipate problems that may arise.

Tours: The new employee is shown how the total company or church works together as a unit and why it is important for all team members to be productive.

Suggested Reading List

Ackoff, Russell Lincoln. *The Art of Problem Solving.* New York: J. Wiley & Sons Publishers, 1978.

Barnett, Homer G. *Innovation: Basis for Cultural Change.* New York: McGraw-Hill, 1953.

Hickman, Craig R. and Michael A. Silva. *The Workbook for Creating Excellence.* New York: Plume Books, 1986.

Hummel, Charles E. *Tyranny of the Urgent.* Downers Grove, Ill.: Inter-Varsity Press, 1967.

Kastens, Merritt. *Long-Range Planning for Your Business.* New York: Amacon, 1976.

Mains, David. *Full Circle.* Waco: Word Books, 1971.

Malkin, Lawrence. *The National Debt.* New York: New American Library, 1988.

Maltz, Maxwell. *Psycho-Cybernetics.* New York: Prentice-Hall, 1960.

Pinchot, Gifford. *Intra-preneuring.* New York: Harper & Row, 1985.

Waddington, C.H. *Tools for Thought.* New York: Basic Books, 1977.

Wiersbe, Warren W. *Be Confident.* Wheaton: Victor Books, 1982.

Yohn, Rick. *Discover Your Spiritual Gift and Use It.* Wheaton: Tyndale House Publishers, 1975.

Zimbardo, Phillip and Ebbe B. Ebbeson. *Influencing Attitudes and Changing Behavior.* Reading, Mass.: Addison-Wesley, 1970.